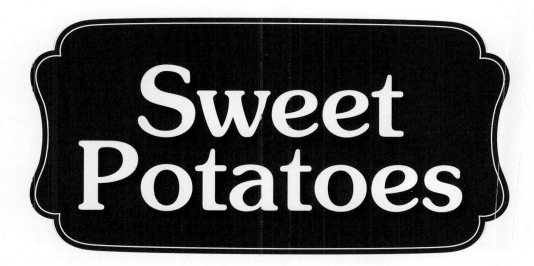

Sweet Potatoes

Publications International, Ltd.

Pictured on the front cover: Glazed Ham and Sweet Potato Kabobs *(page 47)*.

Pictured on the back cover *(top to bottom):* Pecan-Crusted Sweet Potato Cheesecake *(page 12),* Quinoa with Roasted Vegetables *(page 58)* and Creamy Sweet Potato and Butternut Squash Soup *(page 32).*

ISBN: 978-1-4508-5394-1

Manufactured in China.

8 7 6 5 4 3 2 1

Microwave Cooking: Microwave ovens vary in wattage. Use the cooking times as guidelines and check for doneness before adding more time.

Preparation/Cooking Times: Preparation times are based on the approximate amount of time required to assemble the recipe before cooking, baking, chilling or serving. These times include preparation steps such as measuring, chopping and mixing. The fact that some preparations and cooking can be done simultaneously is taken into account. Preparation of optional ingredients and serving suggestions is not included.

Publications International, Ltd.

Happy Holidays

Spirited Sweet Potato Casserole

2½ pounds sweet potatoes
2 tablespoons butter
⅓ cup milk
¼ cup packed brown sugar
2 tablespoons bourbon or apple juice
1 teaspoon ground cinnamon
1 teaspoon vanilla
2 egg whites
½ teaspoon salt
⅓ cup chopped pecans
Whole pecans (optional)

1. Preheat oven to 375°F. Bake potatoes 50 to 60 minutes or until very tender. Cool 10 minutes. Spray 1½-quart soufflé dish with nonstick cooking spray.

2. Scoop pulp from warm potatoes into large bowl; discard potato skins. Add butter to bowl; mash until potatoes are fairly smooth and butter is melted. Stir in milk, brown sugar, bourbon, cinnamon and vanilla; mix well.

3. Beat egg whites in small bowl with electric mixer at high speed until soft peaks form. Add salt; beat until stiff peaks form. Gently fold egg whites into sweet potato mixture.

4. Spoon sweet potato mixture into prepared dish; sprinkle chopped pecans around edge of dish. Place whole pecans in center of casserole, if desired.

5. Bake 30 to 35 minutes or until soufflé is puffed and pecans are toasted. *Makes 8 servings*

Butter Pecan Sweet Potato Crunch

2 cans (15 ounces each) PRINCELLA® or SUGARY SAM® Cut Sweet Potatoes, drained and mashed

1 can (12 ounces) evaporated milk

1 cup sugar

3 eggs

1 tablespoon cinnamon

1 teaspoon vanilla

½ (18¼-ounce) package yellow cake mix (dry)

1 cup chopped pecans

½ cup (1 stick) butter or margarine, melted

Whipped topping

Preheat oven to 350°F. In large bowl, combine first 6 ingredients. Pour sweet potato mixture into greased 13×9-inch cake pan. Sprinkle dry cake mix on top. Cover with chopped pecans. Drizzle melted butter or margarine on top of pecans. Bake for approximately 1 hour or until center is firm. Chill well. Cut into squares. Serve with whipped topping.

Makes 15 to 20 servings

Sweet Potatoes with Cranberry-Ginger Glaze

2 medium sweet potatoes

½ cup dried cranberries

¼ cup cranberry juice

¼ cup maple syrup

2 slices (⅛ inch thick) fresh ginger

Dash black pepper

1. Pierce sweet potatoes all over with fork. Place on paper towel in microwave. Microwave on HIGH 10 minutes or until soft. Peel and cut potatoes into wedges; place in serving dish.

2. Meanwhile, cook cranberries, juice, syrup, ginger and pepper in small saucepan over low heat 7 to 10 minutes or until syrupy. Discard ginger. Pour over potatoes.

Makes 4 servings

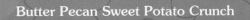

Butter Pecan Sweet Potato Crunch

Sweet Potato, Wild and White Rice Dressing

    ½ cup (1 stick) butter
    2 cups chopped onions
1½ cups chopped celery
    3 cloves garlic, finely chopped
    ½ teaspoon ground ginger
    ½ teaspoon ground sage
    ¼ teaspoon dried rosemary
    ¼ teaspoon ground cinnamon
1½ pounds sweet potatoes, cooked and cut into ½-inch cubes
    1 package (14 ounces) country-style stuffing mix
1½ cups cooked white rice
    1 cup golden raisins
    1 cup toasted pecans, coarsely chopped*
    1 cup cooked wild rice
    ¾ teaspoon salt
    ½ teaspoon black pepper
    1 can (about 14 ounces) chicken broth

To toast pecans, spread in single layer on ungreased baking sheet. Bake in preheated 350°F oven 5 to 7 minutes or until fragrant, stirring occasionally.

1. Preheat oven to 350°F. Grease 13×9-inch baking dish.

2. Melt butter in large nonstick skillet over medium-high heat. Add onions, celery, garlic, ginger, sage, rosemary and cinnamon; cook and stir 6 to 8 minutes or until onions are tender. Transfer to large bowl.

3. Add sweet potatoes, stuffing mix, white rice, raisins, pecans, wild rice, salt and pepper to onion mixture. Toss gently to blend. Drizzle broth over stuffing mixture; toss gently to moisten. Transfer to prepared dish.

4. Cover; bake 30 minutes or until heated through. Uncover; bake 30 minutes or until top is browned.   *Makes 8 servings*

Variation: For alternative to packaged stuffing, place 7 slices of bread directly on oven racks and dry in a 225°F oven for 1 hour. Cut into cubes before using. Makes about 4 cups.

Sweet Potato, Wild and White Rice Dressing

Pecan-Crusted Sweet Potato Cheesecake

Crust
- ¼ cup plus 1 tablespoon unsalted butter, melted
- 1 cup finely crushed gingersnap cookies (about 20 [2-inch] cookies)
- ½ cup chopped pecans, toasted*
- 1 tablespoon sugar
- ⅛ teaspoon salt

Filling
- 4 packages (8 ounces each) cream cheese, softened
- 1¼ cups sugar
- 3 eggs
- 1 can (15 ounces) sweet potatoes in syrup, drained
- 1 cup whipping cream
- 2 teaspoons vanilla
- ½ to 1 tablespoon pumpkin pie spice

*To toast pecans, spread in single layer on ungreased baking sheet. Bake in preheated 350°F oven 5 to 7 minutes or until fragrant, stirring occasionally.

1. Preheat oven to 350°F. Lightly coat 10-inch springform pan with nonstick cooking spray. Wrap double layer of heavy-duty foil around outside of pan.

2. Place crust ingredients in food processor or blender; pulse until mixture resembles coarse crumbs. Press crumbs evenly onto bottom of prepared pan. Bake 8 minutes; place on wire rack to cool slightly.

3. Combine all filling ingredients in food processor or blender; process until smooth. Pour filling into crust. Place springform pan in larger roasting pan or broiler pan. Add enough hot water to come one third up outside of springform pan.

4. Bake 1½ hours or until slightly puffed, softly set and top is golden. Place on wire rack to cool completely. Cover and refrigerate overnight.   *Makes 16 servings*

Pecan-Crusted Sweet Potato Cheesecake

Roasted Sweet Potatoes with Cinnamon & Sweet Onions

    2 pounds sweet potatoes, peeled
    1 sweet onion, cut into eighths
    2 cloves garlic, chopped
    ¼ cup olive oil
    ½ teaspoon ground cinnamon
    2 tablespoons orange juice
      Salt and black pepper

1. Preheat oven to 400°F. Cut potatoes in half lengthwise, then into 1-inch-thick slices.

2. Place potatoes, onion and garlic in 12×8-inch baking dish.

3. Combine olive oil and cinnamon in small bowl; pour over potato mixture. Sprinkle with orange juice, salt and pepper; toss until well coated.

4. Cover; bake 35 to 40 minutes or until potatoes are tender.   *Makes 6 servings*

 Tip: Choose sweet potatoes that are heavy for their size, firm, smooth and free of bruises or blemishes. Check for decay, which often begins at the tips.

Roasted Sweet Potatoes with Cinnamon & Sweet Onions

Sweet Potato Pecan Pie

1 can (16 ounces) sweet potatoes, drained and mashed
3 eggs, divided
¾ cup sugar, divided
1 teaspoon cinnamon
½ teaspoon ground nutmeg
¼ teaspoon ground ginger
  Easy Pie Crust (page 17) *or* 1 (9-inch) frozen deep-dish pie crust*
⅔ cup KARO® Light or Dark Corn Syrup
2 tablespoons margarine or butter, melted
½ teaspoon vanilla
1 cup chopped pecans

To use prepared frozen 9-inch deep-dish pie crust: Do not thaw. Preheat oven and a cookie sheet. Pour filling into frozen crust; bake on cookie sheet.

1. Preheat oven to 350°F.

2. In medium bowl, combine sweet potatoes, 1 egg, ¼ cup sugar, cinnamon, nutmeg and ginger; stir until well blended. Spread evenly in bottom of pie crust.

3. In same bowl, combine remaining 2 eggs, ½ cup sugar, corn syrup, margarine and vanilla; stir until well combined. Stir in pecans. Spoon over sweet potato mixture.

4. Bake 60 minutes or until puffed and set. Cool completely on wire rack.   *Makes 8 servings*

Prep Time: 20 minutes
Bake Time: 60 minutes, plus cooling

Easy Pie Crust

2½ cups flour
1½ teaspoons salt
⅔ cup MAZOLA® Corn Oil
6 tablespoons cold water
½ teaspoon vanilla
1 cup chopped pecans

1. In large bowl, mix flour and salt. Pour oil and water into measuring cup; do not stir. Add liquids all at once to flour mixture. Stir with fork just until moistened. Divide dough into 2 balls.

2. Roll each ball between two sheets of waxed paper, forming a circle approximately 12 inches in diameter.* Remove top sheet of waxed paper; place hand under bottom sheet of paper and invert pastry into pie plate. (Take care not to stretch pastry as this will cause shrinkage.) Trim pastry ½ inch beyond edge of pie plate; fold extra pastry under (even with edge of pie plate). Flute edge with tines of fork or by creating a scallop pattern using fingers.

3. Bake as directed in pie recipe.

Makes two 9-inch single crust pie pastries or 1 double crust pie pastry

*Dampen work area by wiping with a wet dish cloth to prevent wax paper from slipping.

Candied Sweet Potatoes

1½ to 2 pounds sweet potatoes, peeled and sliced into rounds
⅓ cup plus 1½ tablespoons sugar
½ cup water
¼ cup (½ stick) butter
1 tablespoon vanilla
1 teaspoon nutmeg

1. Place potatoes in large saucepan. Sprinkle with sugar. Add water, butter, vanilla and nutmeg; bring to a boil.

2. Reduce heat to medium. Cover; cook 20 to 25 minutes or until potatoes are tender and cooking liquid becomes syrupy.

Makes 6 servings

Two-Toned Stuffed Potatoes

2¼ pounds baking potatoes

1½ pounds sweet potatoes, dark flesh preferred

3 slices thick-cut bacon, cut in half crosswise diagonally

2 cups chopped onions

⅔ cup buttermilk

¼ cup (½ stick) butter, cut into small pieces

¾ teaspoon salt, divided

1. Preheat oven to 450°F. Pierce sweet potatoes all over with fork. Bake directly on rack 45 minutes or until fork-tender. Let potatoes stand until cool enough to handle. *Reduce oven temperature to 350°F.*

2. Meanwhile, cook bacon in medium skillet over medium-high heat 6 to 8 minutes or until crisp. Remove from heat; transfer bacon to paper towels.

3. Add onions to drippings in skillet; cook 12 minutes over medium-high heat or until golden brown. Remove onions from skillet; set aside. Stir buttermilk into skillet, scraping up any browned bits from bottom of pan. Add butter; stir until melted.

4. Cut baking potatoes in half lengthwise; scoop pulp into large bowl. Reserve skins. Add three fourths buttermilk mixture, ½ teaspoon salt and three fourths onions to bowl; mash with potato masher until smooth.

5. Cut sweet potatoes in half lengthwise; scoop pulp into medium bowl. Discard skins. Add remaining buttermilk mixture, ¼ teaspoon salt and one fourth onions to bowl; mash with potato masher until smooth.

6. Fill half of each reserved potato skin with baked potato mixture; fill other half with sweet potato mixture. Top each stuffed potato half with bacon slice. Transfer stuffed potatoes to baking sheet; bake 15 minutes or until heated through.   *Makes 6 servings*

 **Tip:** These stuffed potatoes can be made and frozen weeks in advance. Reheat the frozen potatoes in a preheated 350°F oven for 75 to 90 minutes. If the potatoes are made ahead and refrigerated for a few days, reheat them in a preheated 350°F oven about 25 minutes.

Two-Toned Stuffed Potatoes

Sweet Potato Latkes with Cranberry Compote

    1½ cups fresh cranberries
    ½ cup orange juice
    ¼ cup water
    ¼ cup brandy
    2 tablespoons brown sugar
        Peel of 1 orange
    ½ cinnamon stick
    4 peppercorns, cracked
    2 whole cloves
    1 pound uncooked sweet potatoes, peeled and shredded
    2 eggs
    ¼ cup all-purpose flour
    1 small leek, thinly sliced
    ¼ cup matzo meal
        Salt and black pepper
    ¼ cup olive oil

1. Cook cranberries, orange juice, water, brandy, brown sugar, orange peel, cinnamon stick, peppercorns and cloves in large saucepan over medium-low heat 25 minutes or until cranberries pop and liquid is slightly reduced.

2. Meanwhile, combine sweet potatoes, eggs, flour, leek, matzo meal, salt and black pepper in large bowl until well blended.

3. Heat oil in large skillet over high heat. Flatten about 2 tablespoons batter into pancakes and gently place in oil. Cook latkes 2 minutes per side or until browned. Drain on paper towels. Serve with cranberry compote.

Makes 7 servings

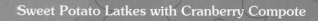
Sweet Potato Latkes with Cranberry Compote

Pumpkin-Sweet Potato Pie with Savory Whipped Cream

1 refrigerated pie crust (half of a 15-ounce package)

2 cups lightly mashed, cooked sweet potatoes*

1 can (15 ounces) solid-pack pumpkin

1 can (14 ounces) sweetened condensed milk

3 eggs

¼ cup (½ stick) butter, cut in small pieces

2 teaspoons Chinese five-spice powder

1½ teaspoons freshly grated lemon peel

Savory Whipped Cream (recipe follows)

*You may substitute canned sweet potatoes.

1. Preheat oven to 350°F. Line 10-inch deep-dish pie plate with pie crust.

2. Combine sweet potatoes, pumpkin, sweetened condensed milk, eggs, butter, five-spice powder and lemon peel in food processor or blender; process until smooth.

3. Pour mixture into pie shell; place on baking sheet. Bake 55 minutes or until puffed and knife inserted 1 inch from center comes out clean. Serve with Savory Whipped Cream.

Makes 8 servings

Savory Whipped Cream

1 cup whipping cream

2 teaspoons lemon peel

¼ teaspoon finely ground black pepper

1 tablespoon lemon juice

1 tablespoon plus 1½ teaspoons bourbon (optional)

Beat cream, lemon peel and pepper in large bowl until soft peaks form. Beat in lemon juice and bourbon, if desired.

Makes 8 servings

Variation: For a more traditional sweet potato marshmallow combination, serve marshmallow cream in place of Savory Whipped Cream.

Pumpkin-Sweet Potato Pie with Savory Whipped Cream

Soups & Stews

Jerk Pork and Sweet Potato Stew

- 2 tablespoons all-purpose flour
- ¼ teaspoon salt
- ¼ teaspoon black pepper
- 1¼ pounds pork shoulder, cut into bite-size pieces
- 2 tablespoons vegetable oil
- 1 large sweet potato, peeled and diced
- 1 cup corn
- 4 tablespoons minced green onions, divided
- 1 clove garlic, minced
- ½ medium Scotch bonnet chile or jalapeño pepper,* cored, seeded and minced
- ⅛ teaspoon ground allspice
- 1 cup chicken broth
- 1 tablespoon lime juice
- 2 cups hot cooked rice

*Scotch bonnet chiles and jalapeño peppers can sting and irritate the skin, so wear rubber gloves when handling and do not touch your eyes.

Slow Cooker Directions

1. Combine flour, salt and pepper in large resealable food storage bag. Add pork; shake well to coat. Heat oil in large skillet over medium heat. Working in batches, add pork in single layer and brown on all sides, about 5 minutes. Transfer to slow cooker.

2. Add sweet potato, corn, 2 tablespoons green onions, garlic, chile and allspice. Stir in broth. Cover; cook on LOW 5 to 6 hours.

3. Stir in lime juice and remaining 2 tablespoons green onions. Serve with rice.

Makes 4 servings

Sweet Potato and Ham Soup

   1 tablespoon butter
   1 leek, sliced
   1 clove garlic, minced
   4 cups chicken broth
   2 sweet potatoes, peeled and cut into ¾-inch cubes
   ½ pound ham, cut into ½-inch cubes
   ½ teaspoon dried thyme
   2 ounces stemmed spinach, coarsely chopped

1. Melt butter in large saucepan over medium heat. Add leek and garlic; cook and stir until tender.

2. Add broth, sweet potatoes, ham and thyme; bring to a boil over high heat. Reduce heat to low; simmer 10 minutes or until sweet potatoes are tender.

3. Stir spinach into soup; simmer 2 minutes or until wilted.
Makes 6 servings

Autumn Beef and Cider Stew

   2 pounds beef for stew, cut into 1- to 1½-inch pieces
   2 slices bacon, cut into ½-inch pieces
   1 teaspoon salt
 ½ teaspoon pepper
   1 can (10½ ounces) condensed French onion soup
   1 cup apple cider
   1 pound sweet potatoes, peeled, cut into 1-inch pieces (about 3 cups)
 ⅓ cup sweetened dried cranberries

1. Cook bacon in stockpot over medium heat until crisp; remove with slotted spoon to paper towel-lined plate. Brown ½ of beef in bacon drippings over medium heat; remove from stockpot. Repeat with remaining beef; season with salt and pepper.

2. Return beef and bacon to stockpot. Add soup and cider; bring to a boil. Reduce heat; cover tightly and simmer 1¾ hours.

3. Add sweet potatoes and cranberries to stockpot; bring to a boil. Reduce heat; continue simmering, covered, 20 to 30 minutes or until beef and potatoes are fork-tender.
Makes 4 to 6 servings

Favorite recipe *Courtesy The Beef Checkoff*

Sweet Potato and Ham Soup

Groundnut Soup with Ginger and Cilantro

    1 tablespoon vegetable oil
1½ cups chopped onions
    1 medium clove garlic, minced
    2 teaspoons chili powder
    1 teaspoon ground cumin
    ¼ teaspoon red pepper flakes
    3 cups chicken broth
    1 can (about 14 ounces) diced tomatoes, undrained
    ½ pound sweet potatoes, peeled and cut into ½-inch cubes
    1 medium carrot, peeled and cut into ½-inch pieces
    2 teaspoons sugar
    1 cup salted peanuts
    1 tablespoon grated fresh ginger
    ¼ cup chopped fresh cilantro

1. Heat oil in large saucepan over medium-high heat. Add onions; cook and stir 4 minutes or until translucent. Add garlic, chili powder, cumin and red pepper flakes; cook and stir 15 seconds.

2. Add broth, tomatoes, sweet potatoes, carrot and sugar; bring to a boil over high heat. Reduce heat; cover tightly and simmer 25 minutes or until vegetables are tender, stirring occasionally. Remove from heat. Stir in peanuts and ginger. Cool slightly.

3. Working in batches, process soup in food processor or blender until smooth. Return to saucepan. Heat over medium-high heat 2 minutes or until heated through. Sprinkle cilantro over each serving.

Makes 4 servings

Yellow Couscous

    1 tablespoon olive oil
    5 green onions, sliced
1⅔ cups water
    ¼ teaspoon salt
    ⅛ teaspoon saffron threads *or* ½ teaspoon ground turmeric
    1 cup uncooked couscous

Heat oil in medium saucepan over medium heat. Add green onions; cook and stir 4 minutes. Add water, salt and saffron; bring to a boil. Stir in couscous. Remove from heat. Cover; let stand 5 minutes.

Makes 3 cups

Jamaican Black Bean Stew

  2 pounds sweet potatoes, peeled and cut into ¾-inch chunks
  3 pounds butternut squash, peeled and seeded
  1 can (about 14 ounces) vegetable broth
  1 large onion, coarsely chopped
  3 cloves garlic, minced
  1 tablespoon curry powder
1½ teaspoons ground allspice
  ½ teaspoon ground red pepper
  ¼ teaspoon salt
  2 cans (15 ounces each) black beans, rinsed and drained
  ½ cup raisins
  3 tablespoons lime juice
    Hot cooked brown rice
  1 cup diced tomato
  1 cup diced peeled cucumber

1. Combine sweet potatoes, squash, broth, onion, garlic, curry powder, allspice, red pepper and salt in Dutch oven; bring to a boil. Reduce heat to low. Cover and simmer 15 minutes or until sweet potatoes and squash are tender. Add beans and raisins; simmer 5 minutes or until heated through. Stir in lime juice.

2. Serve stew over rice; top with tomato and cucumber. *Makes 8 servings*

West African Vegetable Soup

    2 tablespoons olive oil
    1 large sweet onion, sliced (about 2 cups)
    2 cloves garlic, minced
    4 cups SWANSON® Vegetable or Chicken Broth (Regular or Certified Organic)
    ½ teaspoon ground cinnamon
    ½ teaspoon crushed red pepper
    2 medium sweet potatoes, peeled, cut in half lengthwise and sliced (2 cups)
    1 can (14.5 ounces) diced tomatoes, undrained
    ½ cup raisins
    1 bag (6 ounces) spinach, stemmed and coarsely chopped (about 4 cups)
    1 can (about 16 ounces) chickpeas (garbanzo beans), rinsed and drained
    Cooked couscous (optional)

1. Heat the oil in a 6-quart saucepot over medium heat. Add the onion and garlic and cook until tender.

2. Add the broth, cinnamon, red pepper, sweet potatoes, tomatoes and raisins. Heat to a boil. Reduce the heat to low. Cover and cook for 20 minutes or until the potatoes are tender.

3. Add the spinach and chickpeas. Cook until the spinach wilts.

4. Divide soup among **6** serving bowls. Place about **½ cup** of the couscous on top of **each** bowl of soup, if desired.   *Makes 6 servings*

Prep Time: 15 minutes
Cook Time: 30 minutes

West African Vegetable Soup

Creamy Sweet Potato and Butternut Squash Soup

  1 pound sweet potatoes, peeled and cut into 1-inch cubes
  1 pound butternut squash, peeled and diced into 1-inch cubes (about 3½ cups total)
  ½ cup chopped onion
  1 can (about 14 ounces) chicken broth, divided
  ½ cup (1 stick) butter, cubed
  1 can (13½ ounces) coconut milk
1½ teaspoons salt
  ½ teaspoon ground cumin
  ½ teaspoon ground red pepper
  3 to 4 green onions, finely chopped (optional)

Slow Cooker Directions

1. Combine sweet potatoes, squash, onion, half of broth and butter in 4½-quart slow cooker. Cover; cook on HIGH 4 hours or until vegetables are tender.

2. Working with 1 cup at a time, process sweet potato mixture in food processor or blender until smooth; return to slow cooker. Stir in remaining broth, coconut milk, salt, cumin and red pepper. Sprinkle each serving with green onions, if desired. *Makes 4 to 6 servings*

Veal Stew with Horseradish

  1¼ pounds veal, cut into 1-inch cubes
  2 medium sweet potatoes, peeled and cut into 1-inch pieces
  1 can (about 14 ounces) diced tomatoes
  1 package (10 ounces) frozen corn
1½ cups frozen lima beans
  1 large onion, chopped
  1 cup beef or vegetable broth
  1 tablespoon chili powder
  1 tablespoon prepared horseradish
  1 tablespoon honey

Slow Cooker Directions

1. Combine veal, sweet potatoes, tomatoes, corn, lima beans, onion, broth, chili powder, horseradish and honey in 4-quart slow cooker.

2. Cover; cook on LOW 7 to 8 hours or until veal is tender. *Makes 6 servings*

Creamy Sweet Potato and Butternut Squash Soup

Roasted Vegetable Soup

  1 small (about 2 pounds) butternut squash, peeled, seeded and cut into 1½-inch pieces
  3 cups (1 large) peeled and very coarsely chopped sweet potato
  1 cup (1 large) peeled and thickly sliced parsnip
  1 cup (1 medium) thickly sliced leek (white and pale green parts only)
  3 large cloves garlic, peeled
  2 tablespoons extra virgin olive oil
  2 teaspoons MAGGI® Granulated Chicken Flavor Bouillon
  3 cups water, *divided*
  1 can (12 fluid ounces) NESTLÉ® CARNATION® Evaporated Fat Free Milk
¼ teaspoon crushed red pepper
¼ to ½ teaspoon finely chopped fresh sage
    Roasted pepitas (optional)

PREHEAT oven to 425°F. Line shallow roasting pan with foil.

PLACE squash, sweet potato, parsnip, leek and garlic in pan; drizzle with oil. Sprinkle with bouillon; toss to coat.

BAKE for 15 minutes; stir. Bake for an additional 10 to 15 minutes or until tender.

PURÉE *half* of roasted vegetables with about *1½ cups* water in food processor or blender; cover and process until smooth or until desired consistency. Add more water as needed for processing. Pour into large saucepan. Repeat with *remaining* vegetables and *remaining* water.

STIR in evaporated milk, crushed red pepper and sage. Heat over medium-high heat until heated through. Serve with pepitas sprinkled over top.

Makes 4 main-dish or 8 side-dish servings

Prep Time: 25 minutes
Cooking Time: 30 minutes

Caribbean Sweet Potato & Bean Stew

1 pound sweet potatoes, peeled and cut into 1-inch cubes

2 cups frozen cut green beans

1 can (about 15 ounces) black beans, rinsed and drained

1 can (about 14 ounces) vegetable broth

1 small onion, sliced

2 teaspoons Caribbean jerk seasoning

½ teaspoon dried thyme

¼ teaspoon salt

¼ teaspoon ground cinnamon

⅓ cup slivered almonds, toasted*

Hot pepper sauce (optional)

To toast almonds, spread in single layer in heavy skillet. Cook over medium heat 1 to 2 minutes or until nuts are lightly browned, stirring frequently.

Slow Cooker Directions

1. Combine sweet potatoes, green beans, black beans, broth, onion, jerk seasoning, thyme, salt and cinnamon in slow cooker. Cover; cook on LOW 5 to 6 hours or until vegetables are tender.

2. Serve with almonds and hot pepper sauce, if desired.   *Makes 4 servings*

 Tip: To make cleanup easier, spray the inside of the slow cooker with nonstick cooking spray before adding the stew ingredients.

Apple and Chicken Soup

½ pound sweet potatoes
1 tablespoon olive oil
2 stalks celery, thinly sliced
½ medium onion, chopped
1 teaspoon dried thyme
½ teaspoon dried rosemary
¼ teaspoon dried sage
¼ teaspoon ground nutmeg
2 cans (about 14 ounces each) chicken broth
1 cup apple juice
1 large McIntosh apple, peeled and chopped
⅔ cup uncooked small pasta shells
¾ pound boneless skinless chicken breasts, cut into ¼-inch strips

1. Pierce sweet potatoes all over with fork. Place on paper towel in microwave. Microwave on HIGH 5 to 6 minutes or until crisp-tender.

2. Heat oil in large saucepan over medium-high heat. Add celery, onion, thyme, rosemary, sage and nutmeg; cook, covered, 3 minutes or until onion is tender. Add broth, juice and apple; bring to a boil. Stir in pasta; cook, uncovered, 8 to 10 minutes.

3. Meanwhile, peel skin from sweet potato; cut into 1-inch pieces. Add chicken and sweet potatoes to soup. Reduce heat to medium; simmer 5 minutes or until chicken is cooked through and pasta is tender.

Makes 4 to 6 servings

Apple and Chicken Soup

Asian Sweet Potato and Corn Stew

  1 tablespoon vegetable oil
  1 large onion, chopped
  2 tablespoons peeled and minced fresh ginger
  ½ jalapeño or serrano pepper,* seeded and minced
  2 cloves garlic, minced
  1 cup drained canned or thawed frozen corn kernels
  2 teaspoons curry powder
  1 can (13½ ounces) coconut milk
  1 teaspoon cornstarch
  1 can (about 14 ounces) vegetable broth
  1 tablespoon soy sauce, plus additional for seasoning
  4 sweet potatoes, peeled and cut into ¾-inch cubes
    Hot cooked jasmine or long-grain rice
    Chopped cilantro, dry roasted peanuts and green onions (optional)

Jalapeño and serrano peppers can sting and irritate the skin, so wear rubber gloves when handling peppers and do not touch your eyes.

Slow Cooker Directions

1. Heat oil in large skillet over medium heat; add onion, ginger, jalapeño and garlic. Cook 5 minutes or until onion softens, stirring occasionally. Remove from heat and stir in corn and curry powder.

2. Whisk coconut milk and cornstarch together in small cup; stir into slow cooker. Stir in broth and soy sauce. Add sweet potatoes and top with corn mixture. Cover; cook on LOW 5 to 6 hours or until sweet potatoes are tender.

3. Stir gently to smooth cooking liquid without breaking up sweet potatoes. Adjust seasoning with additional soy sauce. Spoon over rice in serving bowls and sprinkle with cilantro, if desired.

Makes 6 servings

Asian Sweet Potato and Corn Stew

Main Courses

Sweet Potato Shepherd's Pie

1 pound sweet potatoes, peeled and cubed

1 pound russet potatoes, peeled and cubed

¼ cup milk

¾ teaspoon salt

1 pound ground turkey

2 packages (4 ounces each) sliced mixed mushrooms *or*
    8 ounces sliced cremini mushrooms

1 jar (12 ounces) beef gravy

½ teaspoon dried thyme

¼ teaspoon black pepper

¾ cup frozen baby peas, thawed

1. Place sweet potatoes and potatoes in medium saucepan. Cover with water and bring to a boil. Reduce heat and simmer, covered, 20 minutes or until potatoes are very tender; drain. Mash potatoes; stir in milk and salt.

2. Meanwhile, preheat broiler. Crumble turkey into large nonstick ovenproof skillet; add mushrooms. Cook and stir over medium-high heat until turkey is no longer pink; drain. Return turkey mixture to skillet. Add gravy, thyme and pepper; simmer 5 minutes. Stir in peas; cook until heated through. Remove skillet from heat.

3. Spread potato mixture over turkey mixture. Broil 4 to 5 inches from heat source 5 minutes or until mixture is hot and topping is lightly browned.   *Makes 6 servings*

Espresso-Bourbon Steaks with Mashed Sweet Potatoes

4 beef tenderloin steaks, cut 1 inch thick (about 4 ounces *each*)
  Mashed Sweet Potatoes (recipe follows)
2 to 4 teaspoons coarsely cracked black pepper
  Steamed green beans

Espresso-Bourbon Sauce:
  ¼ cup bourbon
  ¼ cup maple syrup
  ¼ cup reduced sodium soy sauce
   1 tablespoon fresh lemon juice
   2 teaspoons instant espresso coffee powder
  ⅛ teaspoon black pepper

1. Combine all sauce ingredients except pepper in small saucepan; bring to a boil. Reduce heat and simmer, uncovered, 12 to 15 minutes or until sauce is thickened and reduced by about half, stirring occasionally. Stir in pepper. Keep warm.

2. Prepare Mashed Sweet Potatoes.

3. Meanwhile, press coarsely cracked pepper on both sides of beef steak. Place steaks on grid over medium, ash-covered coals. Grill, uncovered, 13 to 15 minutes (over medium heat on preheated gas grill, covered, 11 to 15 minutes) for medium rare (145°F) to medium (160°F) doneness, turning occasionally.

4. Evenly divide sauce onto 4 plates. Place steak on top of sauce. Serve with Mashed Sweet Potatoes and green beans.   *Makes 4 servings*

Mashed Sweet Potatoes: Place 9 ounces peeled and cubed sweet potatoes and 1 teaspoon salt in large saucepan. Cover with water; bring to a boil. Cook 4 to 5 minutes or until potatoes are tender. Drain. Combine potatoes, 2 tablespoons butter, ⅛ teaspoon salt and ⅛ teaspoon black pepper. Beat until mashed and smooth.

Tip: To broil, place steaks on rack in broiler pan so surface of beef is 2 to 3 inches from heat. Broil 13 to 16 minutes for medium rare to medium doneness, turning once.

Favorite recipe *Courtesy The Beef Checkoff*

Espresso-Bourbon Steaks with Mashed Sweet Potatoes

Tilapia with Tomato Ragoût on Shredded Sweet Potatoes

    2 tablespoons all-purpose flour
    ¼ teaspoon red pepper flakes
    4 tilapia fillets (about 1 pound)
    2 tablespoons olive oil, divided
    6 cups water
    ¾ pound sweet potatoes, peeled and shredded
    ¼ teaspoon salt
      Black pepper (optional)
    ¼ cup diced red onion
    2 cloves garlic, minced
 1½ cups diced plum tomatoes (about 4)
    ¼ cup finely chopped fresh parsley
    2 tablespoons capers, rinsed and drained

1. Combine flour and red pepper flakes in shallow dish. Add tilapia; toss to coat.

2. Heat 1 tablespoon oil in large nonstick skillet over medium-high heat. Place tilapia in skillet; cook 4 to 6 minutes or until fish flakes easily when tested with fork, turning once. Remove from skillet; keep warm.

3. Meanwhile, bring water to a boil in large saucepan. Add sweet potatoes and simmer 5 minutes or just until tender; drain. Add salt and pepper, if desired.

4. Heat remaining 1 tablespoon oil in same skillet over medium-high heat. Add red onion and garlic; cook and stir 30 seconds. Add tomato, parsley and capers; heat through. Divide shredded potatoes among plates. Place tilapia on potatoes; top with tomato ragoût.

Makes 4 servings

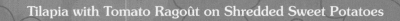
Tilapia with Tomato Ragoût on Shredded Sweet Potatoes

Warm Australian Lamb Salad
with Sweet Potato

1 leg of Australian Lamb, butterflied (see Note)
   Sea salt and freshly ground pepper, to taste

Salad and Dressing
   2 pounds sweet potatoes (2 large or 3 medium)
   2 tablespoons olive oil
   ⅓ cup extra-virgin olive oil
   2 tablespoons red wine or sherry vinegar
      Juice and zest of ½ orange
      Salt and freshly ground pepper, to taste
   2 bunches arugula, torn
   1 small red onion, halved and thinly sliced
   6 ounces of feta cheese, crumbled

1. Trim lamb and season with salt and pepper.

2. Preheat oven to 375°F. Peel and dice the potatoes into ½-inch pieces and toss with the olive oil to coat. Place on a baking sheet and cook for 20 to 30 minutes or until tender and golden brown.

3. Meanwhile, heat grill or grill pan to medium-high and cook lamb for 5 minutes on each side. Cover barbecue or transfer lamb to the oven and cook for 8 to 10 minutes or until medium rare and internal temperature reaches 125 to 130°F. Cover loosely with foil and allow to rest for 15 minutes.

4. To finish the salad while lamb is resting, whisk the dressing ingredients together and season to taste. Toss the arugula, onion and warm potatoes together in a bowl, add half the dressing and mix well. Place on a platter or individual plates. Slice lamb thinly across the grain and arrange over the salad. Scatter with the feta cheese and drizzle with remaining dressing.

Makes 6 servings

Note: To butterfly the lamb, remove netting and open out the leg to make as flat as possible. Pound to desired thinness.

Favorite recipe from *Australian Lamb*

Glazed Ham and Sweet Potato Kabobs

¾ pound sweet potatoes, peeled and cut into 16 pieces
¼ cup water, plus more for soaking skewers
1 boneless ham slice (about 12 ounces), cut into 20 (1-inch) pieces
¼ cup packed dark brown sugar
¼ cup (½ stick) butter
2 tablespoons cider vinegar
2 tablespoons molasses
1 tablespoon yellow mustard
1 tablespoon Worcestershire sauce
¾ teaspoon ground cinnamon
½ teaspoon ground allspice
⅛ teaspoon red pepper flakes
16 fresh pineapple chunks (about 1 inch)
1 package (10 ounces) mixed salad greens

1. Prepare grill for direct cooking over medium heat. Soak 4 (12-inch) wooden skewers in water 20 minutes.

2. Meanwhile, place sweet potatoes in shallow microwavable dish with ¼ cup water. Cover; microwave on HIGH 4 minutes or until fork-tender. Drain. Spread potatoes in single layer; cool 5 minutes.

3. Combine brown sugar, butter, vinegar, molasses, mustard, Worcestershire sauce, cinnamon, allspice and red pepper flakes in large saucepan. Bring to a boil over high heat. Reduce heat to medium-high; cook 2 minutes or until sauce reduces to ½ cup. Remove from heat; cool slightly.

4. Thread ham, potato and pineapple onto prepared skewers, starting and ending with ham. Arrange skewers on oiled grid.

5. Grill 6 to 8 minutes, turning every 2 minutes and brushing with glaze until potatoes are brown and ham is heated through. Cover; let stand 5 minutes.

6. Place salad greens on platter. Remove ham, sweet potato and pineapple from skewers; arrange on top of greens. Serve immediately.   *Makes 4 servings*

Serving Suggestion: Toast 6 to 8 large marshmallows on skewers alongside the kabobs. Separate the sweet potatoes and top with warm marshmallows before serving.

Bean and Vegetable Burritos

2 tablespoons chili powder

2 teaspoons dried oregano

1½ teaspoons ground cumin

1 large sweet potato, peeled and diced

1 can (about 15 ounces) black beans or pinto beans, rinsed and drained

1 medium onion, halved and thinly sliced

1 green bell pepper, chopped

1 cup frozen corn, thawed and drained

4 cloves garlic, minced

1 jalapeño pepper, seeded and minced*

3 tablespoons lime juice

1 tablespoon chopped fresh cilantro

¾ cup (3 ounces) shredded Monterey Jack cheese

4 (10-inch) flour tortillas

Sour cream (optional)

Jalapeño peppers can sting and irritate the skin, so wear rubber gloves when handling peppers and do not touch your eyes.

Slow Cooker Directions

1. Combine chili powder, oregano and cumin in small bowl.

2. Place sweet potato, beans, half of chili powder mixture, onion, bell pepper, corn, garlic and jalapeño pepper in slow cooker. Cover; cook on LOW 5 hours. Stir in lime juice and cilantro.

3. Preheat oven to 350°F. Spoon 2 tablespoons cheese in center of each tortilla. Top with 1 cup filling. Fold all 4 sides to enclose filling. Place burritos, seam sides down, on baking sheet.

4. Cover; bake 20 to 30 minutes or until heated through. Serve with sour cream, if desired.

Makes 4 servings

Bean and Vegetable Burritos

Sweet 'n' Sour Country Ribs

  3 pounds country-style pork ribs, fat trimmed
  3 large sweet potatoes, peeled and cut into 2-inch chunks
  2 cups apple juice
  ¼ cup cider vinegar
  ¼ cup FRENCH'S® Worcestershire Sauce
  ¼ cup packed brown sugar
  2 tablespoons FRENCH'S® Spicy Brown Mustard
  2 tart green apples, cored and cut into 1-inch chunks
  1 tablespoon cornstarch

1. Heat *1 tablespoon oil* in 6-quart saucepot or Dutch oven over high heat. Cook ribs 10 minutes or until well browned on all sides; drain fat.

2. Add sweet potatoes to ribs. Whisk together apple juice, vinegar, Worcestershire, sugar and mustard. Pour over rib mixture; stir well. Heat to boiling. Reduce heat to low. Cook, covered, 40 minutes or until pork is tender and no longer pink in center, stirring occasionally.

3. Stir in apples; cook 5 minutes or until tender. Transfer ribs, sweet potatoes and apples to platter; keep warm. Combine cornstarch with *2 tablespoons water.* Stir into saucepot. Heat to boiling, whisking constantly. Cook 1 to 2 minutes or until liquid thickens, stirring often. Serve with corn and crusty bread, if desired.   *Makes 6 servings (with 2 cups gravy)*

20-Minute Marinade: Marinate 1 pound steak, chicken or chops for 20 minutes in ¼ cup French's® Worcestershire Sauce.

Prep Time: 10 minutes
Cook Time: about 1 hour

Sweet 'n' Sour Country Ribs

Caribbean Stuffed Plantains

    1 pound ground round beef
    3 tablespoons olive oil, divided
1½ cups raw cubed NC sweet potatoes
    1 medium onion, chopped
    1 cup chopped green pepper
  ½ cup sliced celery
    1 large clove garlic, minced
    1 pound canned, chopped tomatoes
    1 tablespoon fresh oregano *or* 1 teaspoon dried oregano
  ½ teaspoon red pepper flakes
  ½ teaspoon seasoned salt
    2 tablespoons chopped parsley
    2 plantains
     Fresh oregano sprigs (optional)
     Pineapple wedges (optional)
     Star fruit (optional)

1. In large skillet, brown beef in 1 tablespoon olive oil. Stir to break into bits. Add sweet potatoes, onion, pepper, celery and garlic. Sauté until vegetables are tender. Add tomatoes, oregano, red pepper, salt and parsley. Simmer 10 minutes to blend flavors.

2. In another skillet, heat remaining 2 tablespoons oil. Slice plantains lengthwise into 4 strips each; sauté in hot oil until golden. Remove from heat and shape into ring. Fasten ends with toothpick. Stand on edge on serving plate. Fill center with sweet potato filling. If desired, garnish with fresh sprigs of oregano, pineapple wedges or star fruit.   *Makes 4 servings*

Favorite recipe from **North Carolina SweetPotato Commission**

Honeyed Harvest Chicken

¾ pound sweet potatoes
4 bone-in chicken breasts
   Salt and black pepper
1 tablespoon olive oil
2 apples, peeled, cored and cut into wedges
¾ cup chicken broth
½ cup dried cranberries
2 tablespoons honey
2 teaspoons lemon juice
⅛ teaspoon ground red pepper
   Hot cooked rice

1. Pierce sweet potato all over with fork. Place on paper towel in microwave. Microwave on HIGH 5 minutes. Peel and cut into 1-inch pieces. Season chicken with salt and black pepper.

2. Heat oil in large skillet over medium-high heat. Add chicken; cook 4 minutes on each side or until brown. Remove chicken to plate; keep warm.

3. Add sweet potato and apples to skillet; cook and stir 2 minutes. Add broth, cranberries, honey, lemon juice and red pepper; bring to a boil. Reduce heat to low. Simmer 2 minutes, stirring occasionally. Return chicken to skillet; simmer 10 minutes or until liquid is thickened and chicken is cooked through (165°F). Serve with rice. *Makes 4 servings*

 **Tip:** To test bone-in chicken pieces for doneness, you should be able to insert a fork into the chicken with ease and the juices should run clear. However, the meat and juices nearest the bones might still be a little pink (not red) even though the chicken is cooked thoroughly.

Maple Salmon and Sweets

    ½ cup pure maple syrup

    2 tablespoons butter, melted

1½ pounds skin-on salmon fillets

    2 medium sweet potatoes, peeled and cut into ½-inch thick slices

       Salt and black pepper

1. Combine maple syrup and butter in measuring cup. Place salmon in large resealable food storage bag. Place sweet potatoes in separate large resealable food storage bag. Pour half of syrup mixture into each bag; seal. Refrigerate at least 2 hours or overnight, turning bags occasionally.

2. Prepare grill for direct cooking. Drain salmon and sweet potatoes; discard marinade. Season with salt and pepper. Grill salmon, skin-side down, on covered grill over medium heat 15 to 20 minutes or until salmon begins to flake when tested with fork. (Do not turn.)

3. Grill sweet potatoes, covered, in single layer on grill topper 15 minutes turning once or twice or until tender and slightly browned. *Makes 4 servings*

Ham and Sweet Potato Skillet

    3 cups water

    1 tablespoon salt

1¼ pounds sweet potatoes, peeled and cut into ¾-inch pieces

    ½ cup brewed coffee

    ¼ cup pure maple syrup

    2 tablespoons butter

    1 fully cooked ham steak (about 1 pound), cut into ¾-inch chunks

    ½ cup coarsely chopped pecans, toasted*

To toast pecans, place in a nonstick skillet. Cook and stir over medium-low heat 5 minutes or until pecans begin to brown. Remove immediately to a plate to cool.

1. Combine water and salt in large saucepan over medium heat. Add sweet potatoes; simmer 8 to 10 minutes or until almost tender. Drain well.

2. Combine coffee, maple syrup and butter in large skillet; bring to a boil over high heat. Reduce heat to medium-low; simmer 3 minutes. Add sweet potatoes and ham; simmer until heated through and sauce is bubbly and slightly thickened, stirring occasionally. Sprinkle with pecans just before serving. *Makes 4 servings*

Maple Salmon and Sweets

Slow-Cooked Autumn Brisket

1 boneless beef brisket (about 3 pounds)

1 small head cabbage (about 1 pound), cut into 8 wedges

1 large sweet potato (about ¾ pound), peeled and cut into 1-inch pieces

1 large onion, cut into 8 wedges

1 medium Granny Smith apple, cored and cut into 8 wedges

2 cans (10¾ ounces each) CAMPBELL'S® Condensed Cream of Celery Soup
    (Regular or 98% Fat Free)

1 cup water

2 teaspoons caraway seed (optional)

Slow Cooker Directions

1. Place the brisket in a 6-quart slow cooker. Top with the cabbage, sweet potato, onion and apple. Stir the soup, water and caraway seed, if desired, in a small bowl. Pour the soup mixture over the brisket and vegetable mixture.

2. Cover and cook on LOW for 8 to 9 hours* or until the brisket is fork-tender. Season as desired. *Makes 8 servings*

*Or on HIGH for 4 to 5 hours.

Prep Time: 20 minutes
Cook Time: 8 hours
Total Time: 8 hours 20 minutes

Slow-Cooked Autumn Brisket

Along Side

Quinoa with Roasted Vegetables

Nonstick cooking spray
2 medium sweet potatoes, cut into ½-inch-thick slices
1 medium eggplant, peeled and cut into ½-inch cubes
1 medium tomato, cut into wedges
1 large green bell pepper, sliced
1 small onion, cut into wedges
½ teaspoon salt
¼ teaspoon black pepper
¼ teaspoon ground red pepper
1 cup uncooked quinoa
2 cloves garlic, minced
½ teaspoon dried thyme
¼ teaspoon dried marjoram
2 cups vegetable broth or water

1. Preheat oven to 450°F. Line 17×12×1-inch jelly-roll pan with foil; spray with cooking spray.

2. Arrange sweet potatoes, eggplant, tomato, bell pepper and onion on prepared pan; spray lightly with cooking spray. Sprinkle with salt, black pepper and ground red pepper; toss to coat. Bake 20 to 30 minutes or until vegetables are browned and tender.

3. Meanwhile, place quinoa in strainer; rinse well. Spray medium saucepan with cooking spray; heat over medium heat. Add garlic, thyme and marjoram; cook and stir 1 to 2 minutes. Add quinoa; cook and stir 2 to 3 minutes. Stir in broth; bring to a boil over high heat. Reduce heat to low. Cover; simmer 15 to 20 minutes or until water is absorbed. (Quinoa will appear somewhat translucent.) Transfer to large bowl; gently stir in roasted vegetables.   *Makes 6 servings*

Beer-Battered Sweet Potato Fries and Onion Rings with Lemon-Thyme Aïoli

Vegetable oil
¾ pound sweet potatoes, cut into ¼-inch-thick matchsticks
2 cups all-purpose flour
1½ cups cornstarch
2 teaspoons baking powder
2 tablespoons paprika
1½ teaspoons salt
¼ teaspoon ground red pepper
2 bottles (12 ounces each) cold lager beer
1 medium onion (about 12 ounces) cut into ½-inch-thick rounds and separated into individual rings
Lemon-Thyme Aïoli (recipe follows)

1. Preheat oven to 200°F. Line one baking sheet with 3 layers of paper towels; set aside. Fill Dutch oven with 3 inches of oil and heat to 350°F. Prepare Lemon-Thyme Aïoli.

2. Place potato pieces in colander and rinse under cold running water. Blot dry with paper towels and set aside.

3. Whisk together flour, cornstarch, baking powder, paprika, salt and red pepper in large bowl. Slowly whisk in beer until completely smooth.

4. Place one third of onion rings in batter and mix gently to coat. Remove from batter one at a time, tapping on side of bowl to shake off excess. Fry in small batches 4 to 5 minutes or until golden brown and crisp, stirring occasionally so rings do not stick together. Drain on prepared baking sheet, then transfer to another baking sheet and keep warm in oven. Repeat with remaining onion rings.

5. Transfer one fourth of the sweet potatoes to batter and mix gently to coat. Remove from batter a few at a time, tapping on side of bowl to shake off excess. Fry in small batches 7 to 8 minutes or until golden brown and crisp, stirring occasionally so fries do not stick together. Drain on prepared baking sheet, then transfer to baking sheet in oven to keep warm. Repeat with remaining fries. Serve with Lemon-Thyme Aïoli. *Makes 4 to 6 servings*

Lemon-Thyme Aïoli: Combine ½ cup mayonnaise, 1 tablespoon water, 1 teaspoon finely grated lemon peel, 2 teaspoons lemon juice, ¼ teaspoon white pepper, ½ teaspoon minced fresh thyme and ⅛ teaspoon minced garlic in small bowl. Makes about ½ cup.

Beer-Battered Sweet Potato Fries and Onion Rings with Lemon-Thyme Aïoli

Jamaican Grilled Sweet Potatoes

1½ pounds sweet potatoes
3 tablespoons packed brown sugar
3 tablespoons melted butter, divided
1 teaspoon ground ginger
1 tablespoon chopped fresh cilantro
2 teaspoons dark rum

1. Prepare grill for direct cooking over medium heat.

2. Pierce sweet potatoes all over with fork. Place on paper towel in microwave. Microwave on HIGH 5 to 6 minutes or until crisp-tender. Diagonally slice potatoes into ¾-inch slices. Combine brown sugar, 1 tablespoon butter and ginger in small bowl; mix well. Stir in cilantro and rum; set aside.

3. Lightly brush one side of each potato slice with half of remaining melted butter. Grill slices, butter side down, on covered grill over medium heat 4 to 6 minutes. Brush tops with remaining melted butter. Turn; grill 3 to 5 minutes. To serve, spoon rum mixture evenly over potato slices.

Makes 6 servings

Mashed Sweet Potatoes with French Meringue

4 egg whites
Pinch cream of tartar
¾ cup sugar
Pinch salt
3 cups mashed, hot sweet potatoes (about 2 pounds uncooked)
2 tablespoons crystallized ginger, finely chopped
1 to 2 tablespoons orange juice
1 tablespoon butter, softened

1. Preheat oven 350°F. Beat egg whites and cream of tartar in large bowl with electric mixer at medium-high speed until soft peaks form. Combine sugar and salt in small bowl; gradually add to egg whites, beating at high speed until stiff peaks form.

2. Combine sweet potatoes, ginger, orange juice and butter in medium bowl; spread in 2-quart casserole. Spread meringue over sweet potatoes. Bake about 14 to 15 minutes or until meringue is golden.

Makes 6 servings

Jamaican Grilled Sweet Potatoes

Mashed Sweet Potatoes & Parsnips

1¼ pounds sweet potatoes, peeled and cut into 1-inch pieces
 2 medium parsnips (about ½ pound), peeled and cut into ½-inch slices
 ¼ cup evaporated milk
1½ tablespoons butter or margarine
 ½ teaspoon salt
 ⅛ teaspoon ground nutmeg
 ¼ cup chopped fresh chives or green onions

1. Combine sweet potatoes and parsnips in large saucepan. Cover with cold water; bring to a boil over high heat. Reduce heat; simmer, uncovered, 15 minutes or until vegetables are tender.

2. Drain vegetables; return to pan. Add milk, butter, salt and nutmeg. Mash potato mixture to desired consistency over low heat. Stir in chives. *Makes 6 servings*

Carrie's Sweet Potato Casserole

 Brown Sugar Topping (recipe follows)
 3 pounds sweet potatoes, cooked and peeled*
 ½ cup (1 stick) butter, softened
 ½ cup granulated sugar
 ½ cup evaporated milk
 2 eggs
 1 teaspoon vanilla
 1 cup chopped pecans

You may substitute canned sweet potatoes.

1. Prepare Brown Sugar Topping.

2. Preheat oven to 350°F. Grease 8 (6-ounce) ovenproof ramekins or 13×9-inch baking dish.

3. Beat sweet potatoes and butter in large bowl with electric mixer at medium speed until light and fluffy. Add granulated sugar, evaporated milk, eggs and vanilla, beating after each addition. Spread evenly in prepared ramekins. Spoon Brown Sugar Topping over sweet potatoes; sprinkle with pecans.

4. Bake 20 to 25 minutes or until set. *Makes 8 to 12 servings*

Brown Sugar Topping: Combine 1 cup packed brown sugar, ½ cup all-purpose flour and ⅓ cup melted butter in medium bowl; mix well.

Mashed Sweet Potatoes & Parsnips

Sweet Potato Gratin

3 pounds sweet potatoes
½ cup (1 stick) butter, divided
¼ cup plus 2 tablespoons packed light brown sugar, divided
⅔ cup orange juice
2 eggs
2 teaspoons ground cinnamon, divided
½ teaspoon salt
¼ teaspoon ground nutmeg
⅓ cup all-purpose flour
¼ cup old-fashioned oats
⅓ cup chopped pecans or walnuts

1. Preheat oven to 350°F.

2. Bake sweet potatoes 1 hour or until tender. Let stand 5 minutes. Cut lengthwise into halves. Scrape pulp from skins into large bowl.

3. Beat sweet potato pulp, ¼ cup butter and 2 tablespoons brown sugar with electric mixer at medium speed until butter is melted. Add orange juice, eggs, 1½ teaspoons cinnamon, salt and nutmeg; beat until smooth. Pour mixture into 6 (6-ounce) ovenproof ramekins or 1½-quart baking dish.

4. Combine flour, oats, remaining ¼ cup brown sugar and ½ teaspoon cinnamon in medium bowl. Cut in remaining ¼ cup butter with pastry blender or two knives until mixture resembles coarse crumbs. Stir in pecans. Sprinkle evenly over sweet potatoes.*

5. Bake 25 to 30 minutes or until heated through. For crispier topping, broil 5 inches from heat source 2 to 3 minutes or until golden brown. *Makes 6 to 8 servings*

At this point, this recipe may be covered and refrigerated up to 1 day. Let stand at room temperature 1 hour before baking.

Sweet Potato Gratin

Rich Roasted Sesame Vegetables

  1 medium carrot, peeled, quartered lengthwise and cut into 2-inch pieces
  ¼ pound sweet potatoes, peeled and cut into ¾-inch cubes
  ½ red bell pepper, cut into 1-inch cubes
  ½ medium onion, cut into ½-inch wedges
  3 teaspoons sesame oil, divided
  2 teaspoons sugar, divided
  ¼ teaspoon salt

1. Preheat oven to 425°F. Line baking sheet with foil. Place carrot, sweet potatoes, bell pepper and onion in single layer on prepared baking sheet. Sprinkle evenly with 2 teaspoons oil, 1 teaspoon sugar and salt; toss gently to coat. Bake 10 minutes. Stir; cook 10 minutes or until edges are richly browned and sweet potatoes are tender.

2. Remove from oven. Sprinkle vegetables with remaining 1 teaspoon oil and 1 teaspoon sugar. Toss gently to coat.   *Makes 2 servings*

Serving Suggestion: Sprinkle vegetables with rice wine vinegar or lime juice just before serving.

Three-Potato Salad

  3 pounds assorted potatoes (all-purpose, red and/or sweet potatoes or yams),
      unpeeled and cut into 1-inch pieces
  ½ cup HELLMANN'S® or BEST FOODS® Real Mayonnaise*
  1 tablespoon Dijon mustard
  ¼ cup sliced green onions
    Salt and ground black pepper (optional)
  4 slices bacon, crisp-cooked and crumbled (optional)
Also terrific with HELLMANN'S® or BEST FOODS® Light Mayonnaise.

Cover potatoes with water in 4-quart saucepot; bring to a boil over high heat. Reduce heat to low and simmer 14 minutes or until potatoes are tender. Drain and cool slightly.

Combine HELLMANN'S® or BEST FOODS® Real Mayonnaise with mustard in large bowl. Add potatoes and onions; toss gently. Season to taste with salt and black pepper. Serve chilled or at room temperature. Just before serving, sprinkle with bacon.   *Makes 12 servings*

Prep Time: 10 minutes
Cook Time: 14 minutes

Rich Roasted Sesame Vegetables

Sweet Potato-Cranberry Bake

1 can (40 ounces) whole sweet potatoes, drained
1⅓ cups FRENCH'S® French Fried Onions, divided
2 cups fresh cranberries
2 tablespoons packed brown sugar
⅓ cup honey

Preheat oven to 400°F. In 1½-quart casserole, layer sweet potatoes, ⅔ cup French Fried Onions and *1 cup* cranberries. Sprinkle with brown sugar; drizzle with *half* the honey. Top with remaining cranberries and honey. Bake, covered, at 400°F for 35 minutes or until heated through. Gently stir casserole. Top with remaining ⅔ cup onions; bake, uncovered, 1 to 3 minutes or until onions are golden brown.   *Makes 4 to 6 servings*

Coconut Butternut Squash

1 tablespoon butter
½ cup chopped onion
1 pound butternut squash, peeled, seeded and cut into 1-inch pieces
1 pound sweet potatoes, peeled and cut into 1-inch pieces
1 can (13½ ounces) coconut milk
3 tablespoons packed light brown sugar, divided
½ teaspoon salt
½ teaspoon ground cinnamon
¼ teaspoon ground nutmeg
¼ teaspoon ground allspice
1 tablespoon grated fresh ginger

1. Melt butter in large skillet over medium-high heat. Add onion; cook and stir 4 minutes or until translucent. Stir in squash, sweet potatoes, coconut milk, 1 tablespoon brown sugar, salt, cinnamon, nutmeg and allspice. Bring to a boil over medium-high heat. Reduce heat; cover and simmer 10 minutes. Uncover; cook 5 minutes or until vegetables are tender, stirring frequently. Remove from heat. Add ginger.

2. Pour into food processor or blender; process until smooth. Sprinkle with remaining 2 tablespoons brown sugar.   *Makes 7 servings*

Sweet Potato-Cranberry Bake

Sweet-Spiced Sweet Potatoes

2 pounds sweet potatoes, peeled and cut into ½-inch pieces
¼ cup packed dark brown sugar
1 teaspoon ground cinnamon
½ teaspoon ground nutmeg
⅛ teaspoon salt
2 tablespoons butter, cut into small pieces
1 teaspoon vanilla

Slow Cooker Directions

1. Combine sweet potatoes, brown sugar, cinnamon, nutmeg and salt in slow cooker; mix well. Cover; cook on LOW 7 hours or on HIGH 4 hours.

2. Add butter and vanilla; gently stir to blend.

Makes 4 servings

Heavenly Sweet Potatoes

Vegetable cooking spray
1 can (40 ounces) cut sweet potatoes in heavy syrup, drained
¼ teaspoon ground cinnamon
⅛ teaspoon ground ginger
¾ cup SWANSON® Chicken Broth (Regular, Natural Goodness® or Certified Organic)
2 cups miniature marshmallows

1. Heat the oven to 350°F.

2. Spray a 1½-quart casserole with cooking spray.

3. Put the potatoes, cinnamon and ginger in an electric mixer bowl. Beat at medium speed until almost smooth. Add the broth and beat until potatoes are fluffy. Spoon the potato mixture in the prepared dish. Top with the marshmallows.

4. Bake for 20 minutes or until heated through and marshmallows are golden brown.

Makes 8 servings

Bake Time: 20 minutes
Prep Time: 10 minutes
Total Time: 30 minutes

Sweet-Spiced Sweet Potatoes

Decadent Desserts

Steamed Southern Sweet Potato Custard

　1 can (16 ounces) cut sweet potatoes, drained
　1 can (12 ounces) evaporated milk, divided
　½ cup packed light brown sugar
　2 eggs, lightly beaten
　1 teaspoon ground cinnamon
　½ teaspoon ground ginger
　¼ teaspoon salt
　　Whipped cream
　　Ground nutmeg

Slow Cooker Directions

1. Place sweet potatoes and ¼ cup evaporated milk in food processor or blender; process until smooth. Add remaining milk, brown sugar, eggs, cinnamon, ginger and salt; process until well blended. Pour into ungreased 1-quart soufflé dish. Cover tightly with foil. Crumple large sheet of foil (about 15×12 inches); place in bottom of slow cooker. Pour 2 cups water over foil. Make foil handles.*

2. Transfer dish to slow cooker using foil handles. Cover; cook on HIGH 2½ to 3 hours or until skewer inserted into center comes out clean.

3. Use foil handles to lift dish from slow cooker; transfer to wire rack. Uncover; let stand 30 minutes. Garnish with whipped cream and nutmeg.　　　　　*Makes 4 servings*

*To make foil handles, tear off 3 (18×3-inch) strips of heavy-duty foil. Crisscross the strips so they resemble the spokes of a wheel. Place the dish in the center of the strips. Pull the foil strips up and over the dish and place it into the slow cooker. Leave the foil strips in while the food cooks, so you can easily lift the item out again when it is finished cooking.

Spiced Sweet Potato Cupcakes

1¼ pounds sweet potatoes, peeled and quartered
1½ cups all-purpose flour
1¼ cups granulated sugar
2 teaspoons baking powder
1 teaspoon ground cinnamon
½ teaspoon baking soda
½ teaspoon salt
¼ teaspoon ground allspice
¾ cup canola or vegetable oil
2 eggs
½ cup chopped walnuts or pecans, plus additional for garnish
½ cup raisins
Cream Cheese Frosting (recipe follows)

1. Place sweet potatoes in large saucepan; add enough water to cover by 1 inch. Cover; cook over medium heat 30 minutes or until fork-tender, adding additional water, if necessary. Drain; mash when cool enough to handle. Measure 2 cups.

2. Preheat oven to 325°F. Line 18 standard (2½-inch) muffin cups with paper baking cups.

3. Whisk flour, sugar, baking powder, cinnamon, baking soda, salt and allspice in medium bowl. Beat sweet potatoes, oil and eggs in large bowl with electric mixer at low speed until blended. Add flour mixture; beat at medium speed 30 seconds or until blended. Stir in ½ cup walnuts and raisins. Spoon batter evenly into prepared muffin cups.

4. Bake 20 minutes or until toothpick inserted into centers comes out clean. Cool completely in pans on wire racks.

5. Meanwhile, prepare Cream Cheese Frosting. Frost cupcakes; sprinkle with additional walnuts. Store covered in refrigerator.   *Makes 18 cupcakes*

Cream Cheese Frosting: Beat 1 package (8 ounces) softened cream cheese and ¼ cup (½ stick) softened butter in medium bowl with electric mixer at medium-high speed until creamy. Gradually beat in 1½ cups sifted powdered sugar until well blended. Beat in ¼ teaspoon salt and ¼ teaspoon vanilla. Makes about 3 cups.

Spiced Sweet Potato Cupcakes

Sweet Potato Coconut Bars

30 vanilla wafers, crushed*
1½ cups finely chopped walnuts, toasted, divided**
 1 cup sweetened flaked coconut, divided
¼ cup (½ stick) butter, softened
 2 cans (16 ounces each) sweet potatoes, well drained and mashed (2 cups)
 2 eggs
 1 teaspoon ground cinnamon
½ teaspoon ground ginger
¼ to ½ teaspoon ground cloves
¼ teaspoon salt
 1 can (14 ounces) sweetened condensed milk
 1 cup butterscotch chips

*Vanilla wafers can be crushed in a food processor or in a large resealable food storage bag with a rolling pin. This is a great way to use up the broken pieces that always end up at the bottom of the bag.

** To toast walnuts, spread in single layer on baking sheet. Bake in preheated 350°F oven 5 to 7 minutes or until fragrant, stirring occasionally.

1. Preheat oven to 350°F.

2. Combine vanilla wafers, 1 cup walnuts, ½ cup coconut and butter in medium bowl until well blended. (Mixture will be dry and crumbly.) Place two thirds of crumb mixture in bottom of 13×9-inch baking pan, pressing down lightly to form even layer.

3. Beat sweet potatoes, eggs, cinnamon, ginger, cloves and salt in large bowl with electric mixer at medium-low speed until well blended. Gradually add sweetened condensed milk; beat until well blended. Spoon filling evenly over crust. Top with remaining crumb mixture, pressing lightly into sweet potato layer.

4. Bake 25 to 30 minutes or until knife inserted into center comes out clean. Sprinkle with butterscotch chips, remaining ½ cup walnuts and ½ cup coconut. Bake 2 minutes. Cool completely in pan on wire rack. Cover and refrigerate 2 hours before serving.

Makes 2 dozen bars

Sweet Potato Coconut Bars

Pecan-Topped Sweet Potato Pie

1 unbaked deep-dish 9-inch pie crust

1½ cups pecan halves

½ cup light corn syrup

1 egg white

2 cups puréed cooked sweet potatoes (about 1½ pounds uncooked)

⅓ cup packed brown sugar

1 teaspoon *each* vanilla and ground cinnamon

¼ teaspoon salt

Pinch *each* ground nutmeg and ground cloves

2 eggs, beaten

1. Preheat oven to 400°F. Prick holes in bottom of crust with fork. Bake 10 minutes or until light brown. Cool completely on wire rack. *Reduce oven temperature to 350°F.*

2. Combine pecans, corn syrup and egg white in small bowl. Combine sweet potatoes, brown sugar, vanilla, cinnamon, salt, nutmeg and cloves in large bowl. Stir in eggs. Spread sweet potato mixture evenly in pie crust. Spoon pecan mixture evenly over top.

3. Bake 45 minutes or until filling is puffed and topping is golden.   *Makes 8 servings*

Gingered Sweet Potato Cake

1 package (about 18 ounces) spice cake mix

1⅓ cups water

1 cup mashed sweet potatoes

6 egg whites

2 tablespoons canola oil

1 tablespoon grated fresh ginger

1 container (8 ounces) whipped topping

1. Preheat oven to 350°F. Coat 13×9-inch baking pan with nonstick cooking spray.

2. Combine cake mix, water, sweet potatoes, egg whites, oil and ginger in large bowl; mix according to package directions. Pour batter into prepared baking pan.

3. Bake 30 minutes or until toothpick inserted into center comes out clean. Cool completely in pan on wire rack. Frost with whipped topping. Cover and refrigerate until ready to serve.

Makes 18 servings

Pecan-Topped Sweet Potato Pie

Nutty Fruit Salad

½ pound sweet potatoes

1 Granny Smith apple, unpeeled and chopped

¼ cup chopped celery

1 container (6 ounces) plain yogurt

1 jalapeño pepper,* seeded and chopped (optional)

2 tablespoons orange juice

½ to 1 teaspoon grated fresh ginger

½ teaspoon curry powder

⅛ teaspoon salt

½ cup cinnamon-coated nuts, divided

¼ cup drained mandarin oranges

*Jalapeño peppers can sting and irritate the skin, so wear rubber gloves when handling peppers and do not touch your eyes.

1. Pierce sweet potatoes all over with fork. Place on paper towel in microwave. Microwave on HIGH 6 to 7 minutes or until crisp-tender.

2. Peel sweet potatoes and cut into 1-inch pieces. Combine sweet potatoes, apple and celery in large bowl. Combine yogurt, jalapeño, orange juice, ginger, curry powder and salt in small bowl. Add to sweet potato mixture; toss to coat. Add half of nuts; stir gently. Top with remaining nuts and oranges. Refrigerate until ready to serve.   *Makes 4 to 6 servings*

Variation: Any type of flavored nut will work great, including honey-roasted or praline-coated varieties.

Sweet Potato Pie

3 large sweet potatoes, peeled and cut into cubes (about 3 cups)

¼ cup heavy cream

1 can (10¾ ounces) CAMPBELL'S® Condensed Tomato Soup

1 cup packed brown sugar

3 eggs

1 teaspoon vanilla extract

½ teaspoon ground cinnamon

½ teaspoon ground nutmeg

1 (9-inch) frozen pie crust

1. Heat the oven to 350°F.

2. Place potatoes into a 3-quart saucepan and add water to cover. Heat over medium-high heat to a boil. Reduce the heat to low. Cover and cook for 10 minutes or until the sweet potatoes are tender. Drain the potatoes well in a colander.

3. Place the sweet potatoes and heavy cream into a large bowl. Beat with an electric mixer on medium speed until the mixture is fluffy. Beat in the soup, brown sugar, eggs, vanilla extract, cinnamon and nutmeg. Pour the potato mixture into the pie crust and place onto a baking sheet.

4. Bake for 1 hour or until set. Cool the pie in the pan on a wire rack about 3 hours.

Makes 8 servings

Kitchen Tip: Substitute 1¾ cups drained and mashed canned sweet potatoes for the fresh mashed sweet potatoes.

Prep Time: 15 minutes
Bake Time: 1 hour
Cool Time: 3 hours

Sweet Potato Phyllo Wraps

¾ cup mashed cooked sweet potato
¾ teaspoon vanilla
½ teaspoon ground cinnamon
4 (16½×12-inch) sheets frozen phyllo dough, thawed
　Nonstick cooking spray
4 tablespoons finely chopped pecans
1 tablespoon light maple syrup
　Fresh strawberries (optional)

1. Preheat oven to 375°F. Line baking sheet with parchment paper.

2. Combine sweet potato, vanilla and cinnamon in small bowl; mix well.

3. Unroll phyllo dough, keeping sheets stacked. Cover with large sheet of waxed paper and damp kitchen towel. Remove one sheet at a time; place on work surface with short side facing you. Spray edges lightly with cooking spray.

4. Spread 3 tablespoons sweet potato mixture across short edge of phyllo dough. Sprinkle with 1 tablespoon pecans. Roll up tightly. Cut into thirds; place on prepared baking sheet. Repeat with remaining phyllo sheets, sweet potato mixture and pecans. Spray tops of wraps with cooking spray.

5. Bake 15 to 20 minutes or until golden brown. Drizzle with maple syrup. Garnish with strawberries, if desired.

Makes 12 wraps

Sweet Potato Phyllo Wraps

Sweet Potato Fool

2 cups cooked, puréed sweet potatoes *or* 1 can (15 ounces) sweet potato purée
¼ cup packed light brown sugar
½ teaspoon ground cinnamon
¼ teaspoon ground ginger
1 cup whipping cream
3 tablespoons powdered sugar
12 gingersnap cookies, coarsely crushed

1. Combine sweet potatoes, brown sugar, cinnamon and ginger in medium bowl, stirring until well blended.

2. Beat cream in large bowl with electric mixer at high speed until thickened. Gradually add powdered sugar; beat until stiff.

3. To assemble, layer half of gingersnaps in 2-quart glass bowl. Spread with half of sweet potato purée and half of whipped cream. Repeat layers. Chill 1 hour before serving.

Makes 6 servings

 Tip: Sweet potatoes need not be peeled, but should be scrubbed under cold running water before cooking. Cooking with skins intact retains more nutrients.

Sweet Potato Fool

Maple-Sweet Potato Cheesecake Pies

 1 package (8 ounces) cream cheese (such as Neufchâtel), softened
½ cup vanilla yogurt
 1 can (16 ounces) sweet potatoes, drained and mashed*
½ cup pure maple syrup
 1 teaspoon vanilla
½ teaspoon ground cinnamon
¼ teaspoon ground cloves
 1 egg
 1 egg white
12 mini graham cracker crusts
    Pecan halves

*Mashing sweet potatoes by hand produces pie filling with a somewhat coarse texture. For a smoother texture, process sweet potatoes in a food processor until smooth.

1. Preheat oven to 350°F.

2. Beat cream cheese in medium bowl with electric mixer at medium speed until creamy. Beat in yogurt, sweet potatoes, maple syrup, vanilla, cinnamon and cloves until smooth. Beat in egg and egg white until combined.

3. Spoon sweet potato mixture evenly into crusts.** Top each with pecan halves. Place pies on large baking sheet.

4. Bake 30 to 35 minutes or until set and knife inserted into centers comes out clean. Cool 1 hour on wire rack. Chill before serving.   *Makes 12 servings*

**You may pour sweet potato mixture into a 9-inch graham cracker crust, if desired. Bake 40 to 45 minutes.

Maple-Sweet Potato Cheesecake Pie

Sweet Potato Cheesecake

2 packages (8 ounces each) cream cheese, softened
¼ cup sugar
¼ cup packed brown sugar
1 teaspoon vanilla
2 eggs
1½ cups puréed cooked sweet potato (about 1 pound uncooked)
½ teaspoon cinnamon
Pinch *each* ground cloves, ground ginger and ground nutmeg
1 (9-inch) graham cracker crust

1. Preheat oven to 350°F.

2. Beat cream cheese in large bowl with electric mixer until smooth. Add sugars and vanilla; beat until well blended. Add eggs, one at a time, beating well after each addition. Add sweet potato purée and beat well. Add spices; mix until well blended. Pour batter into crust.

3. Bake 45 to 50 minutes. Let cool completely before serving.   *Makes 8 servings*

 Tip: A simple doneness test is to gently shake the cheesecake—a 1-inch area in the center of the cheesecake should jiggle slightly. This area will firm during cooling. After baking, run a knife around the inside of the pan to loosen the edges of the crust. Let cool and then remove the rim of the pan. Cheesecakes can be stored in the refrigerator for up to one week, but for the best flavor, bring them to room temperature before serving. Cheesecakes are not recommended for freezing.

Sweet Potato Cheesecake

Sweet Potato Muffins

  2 cups all-purpose flour
¾ cup chopped walnuts
¾ cup golden raisins
½ cup packed brown sugar
  1 tablespoon baking powder
  1 teaspoon ground cinnamon
½ teaspoon salt
½ teaspoon baking soda
¼ teaspoon ground nutmeg
  1 cup mashed cooked sweet potato
¾ cup milk
½ cup (1 stick) butter, melted
  2 eggs, beaten
1½ teaspoons vanilla

1. Preheat oven to 400°F. Grease 24 standard (2½-inch) muffin cups.

2. Combine flour, walnuts, raisins, brown sugar, baking powder, cinnamon, salt, baking soda and nutmeg in medium bowl; stir until well blended.

3. Combine sweet potato, milk, butter, eggs and vanilla in large bowl; stir until well blended. Add flour mixture to sweet potato mixture; stir just until moistened. Spoon batter evenly into prepared muffin cups.

4. Bake 15 minutes or until toothpick inserted into centers comes out clean. Cool in pans 5 minutes. Remove to wire racks; cool completely. *Makes 24 muffins*

The publisher would like to thank the companies and organizations listed below for the use of their recipes and photographs in this publication.

ACH Food Companies, Inc.

Allens®

Australian Lamb

The Beef Checkoff

Campbell Soup Company

Nestlé USA

North Carolina SweetPotato Commission

Reckitt Benckiser LLC.

Unilever